Happiness in Living Color

Inspiration by Ieda Jónasdóttir Herman
Compiled by Heidi Herman

Happiness in Living Color

Inspirational Message Adult Coloring Book

Hekla Publishing LLC
Happiness in Living Color
Adult Coloring Book
ISBN: 978-1-947233-71-3

All rights reserved. No part of this book may be reproduced or transmitted in any form or by any means, electronic or mechanical, including photocopying, recording, or by any information storage and retrieval system, without the written permission of the Author, except where permitted by law

Ieda Jónasdóttir Herman is an Icelandic-born life explorer who inspires many through her vitality, positive attitude, and endless energy.

To those around her, she is known as Viking Amma

These inspirational thoughts and motivational ideas are her foundation for a happy life. May they inspire you as well.

I always try to get a window seat when flying on an airplane. I love to look down on the earth from the angels point of view

My Grandfather's early training and admonition that "Viking kids don't cry" has helped me to have courage and a strong will

Some call it foolhardy and stubborn but it has served me well

We can't live like chickens in a coop and expect to be able to soar the skies like seagulls

I do have a choice when I wake up in the morning.

I can think about the aches and pains; about the troubles of the day….OR, I can choose to be happy.

I choose to be happy.

This is the day The Lord has made, I WILL rejoice and be glad in it.
-Psalm 118:24

When I need to think, I head for water.

A lake, a river, a little pond.

There's something about the water that is peaceful.

Attitude is Everything
Choose to believe

Yes I can ~ Yes you can ~
Yes we can.

Choose a different perspective
to change how you see things

The word "No"
turned upside-down
becomes "On"

I am far to busy enjoying life to be limited by acting my age.

Whatever that means.

Join my adventure or be content to watch ~

Just don't tell me I can't follow my dreams.

Find the Good

The world is filled with heartache, pain, and sadness. There are plenty of mean people, anger, selfishness, and unhappiness.

There is also light, life, and laughter. There are beautiful views everywhere around you if you choose to look and see.

There are also good people. People who care and help others.

If you have trouble finding one, make sure you are one.

The people around you need it.

"Much always longs for more"
-Icelandic Proverb

I have always found I am happiest with what I have when I don't compare it to what others have.

I don't have to keep up with the Jones'—I've taken a different road.

Friends are sometimes like butterflies that come into your life and leave too quickly.

Love them while they are with you.

Yesterday cannot be re-lived and regret serves no purpose

Tomorrow isn't here yet and worry won't solve any problems.

Today is all you have. Live in the moment. Treasure it and make the most of it.

You are not guaranteed that tomorrow will come. If it doesn't, know that you gave your best today.

Be happy, be vibrant. Love yourself and those around you.

Today is the best day to be alive.

Wine & Chocolate

My doctor told me I needed more greens in my diet. On the way home, I stopped and bought my favorite candy-coated chocolate.

Thank goodness there were green ones in there.

Another doctor told me Muscatine grapes were good for me. So, I bought the convenient liquid form.

Who am I to question doctor's orders?

I kept seeing a lot of articles about Yoga and I became interested and added it to my routine. I didn't care that I was over 80. Nothing I read said I shouldn't.

I wanted to share my memories of growing up in Iceland. I wrote my childhood memoirs when I was 85. Nobody told me I couldn't.

I always wanted to fly like the seagulls in Iceland. At 88, my wish came true when I was given the opportunity to go paragliding in Utah. I never once thought I wouldn't.

I should

I can

I will

Every dream is within my power to achieve.

I love reading the insights and thoughts of great minds.

I am so inspired by the writings of Thomas Jefferson, Benjamin Franklin, Eleanor Roosevelt, Winston Churchill, and Thomas Edison.

Who inspires you?

If the way I have lived my life has instilled in my children a zest for life, a thirst for knowledge, and a desire to experience all the world has to offer, then I have done well.

www.ingramcontent.com/pod-product-compliance
Lightning Source LLC
Chambersburg PA
CBHW080028130526
44591CB00037B/2711